Using Social Networks

Bonnie Spivet

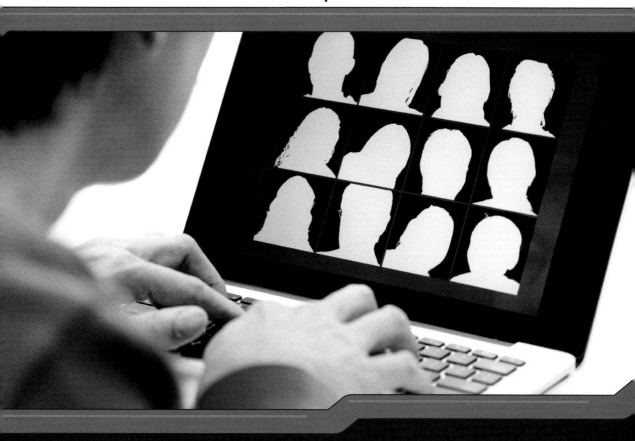

PowerKiDS
press

New York

Published in 2012 by The Rosen Publishing Group
29 East 21st Street, New York, NY 10010

First Edition

Editor: Karolena Bielecki
Book Design: Erica Clendening

Photo credits: Cover © www.istockphoto.com/YinYang; p. 5 © Michael
Haegele/Corbis; p. 6 © www.istockphoto.com/Silvia Boratti; p. 9 © www.
istockphoto.com/Jani Bryson; pp. 11, 21 Thomas Tolstrup/Taxi/Getty Images;
p. 13 Gregory Costanzo/Riser/Getty Images; p. 14 © www.istockphoto.com/
Daniel Laflor; p. 16 Bruce Laurance/The Image Bank/Getty Images; p. 19 ©
LWA-Dann Tardif/Corbis.

Library of Congress Cataloging-in-Publication Data

Spivet, Bonnie.
Using social networks / by Bonnie Spivet.—1st ed.
    p. cm.—(Cybersmarts: staying safe online)
Includes index.
ISBN 978-1-4488-6415-7 (library binding)—ISBN 978-1-4488-6425-6 (pbk.)—
ISBN 978-1-4488-6426-3 (6-pack)
1. Social networks—Juvenile literature. 2. Internet and children—Juvenile
literature. 3. Internet—Safety measures—Juvenile literature. I. Title.
HM741.S654 2012
006.7'54083—dc23
                                                            2011017645

Manufactured in the United States of America

CPSIA Compliance Information: Batch #W12PK: For further information, contact Rosen Publishing, New York, New York, at
1–800–237–9932.

Contents

What Is a Social Network?

You have probably heard of Facebook and Twitter. These popular Web sites are social networks. What is a social network? It is an online community where people are in touch with friends. There are different social networks for all ages. For example, Whyville, Everloop, and Club Penguin are all social networks.

People use social-networking sites in many ways. They share thoughts, talk to friends, and play games. People trade messages about movies, TV shows, and sports on these sites, too. Some social networks even have **apps**. Apps are programs you can download for your mobile phone or tablet. They let you use your social network when you are not at your computer. You can have fun on social networks, but remember to use them safely.

Social-networking sites exist on the Internet so you can visit these communities at any time and from any place. All you need is a computer or mobile device, like a phone or tablet, with an Internet connection.

Find the Right Network

Some social networks are for kids in elementary and middle school. Others, such as Facebook and LinkedIn, are for high-school kids and adults. Most networking sites have **age requirements**. Never pretend to be older than you really are online. Age limits are there to keep kids safe.

There are a lot of different social networks online. Be sure you and your friends use the one that is safest for you.

Talk with a parent or guardian before you sign up for a social network. He can help decide if it is right for you. For example, Togetherville is best for kids 10 years old and younger. It is meant to be like Facebook for younger users. It might seem boring to a kid who just wants to play games, though. No matter your age, there is a safe, fun network that has you and your interests in mind!

Underage Facebooking

Facebook is the largest social network in the world. It has over 600 million users! You must be over 13 years old to use Facebook. Facebook has this rule to comply with the Children's Online Privacy Protection Act (COPPA). COPPA is an American law that stops Web sites from collecting personal information from kids. You should not join Facebook unless you are at least 13 years old. Even then, you should ask a parent's permission. Facebook kicks 20,000 underage users off every day.

Some kids lie about their birthdays. Lying about your age is wrong. It puts you in danger. You could become the target of bad people, like predators. Facebook allows people to share personal information with their friends or the public. It has complicated privacy settings. These may be confusing for a kid to figure out.

Until you turn 13, though, there are a lot of cool Facebook-style social networks, like Togetherville. It has the same look and feel as Facebook but is for younger users.

Games and More

Social networks are great places to play games. Sites such as Skid-e-Kids, Disney's ToonTown, and Moshi Monsters offer all sorts of different games. Some games even help teach reading and math. Many of the games on social-networking sites are played alone. Others, called multiplayer games, are played by big groups of people.

However, networking sites have more than games. Many social networks can be your home base online. From your profile page, you can send messages, write stories, and learn to connect with people using a computer. These activities can be great problem-solving tools and teach you to be **responsible** online.

Ask your friends which social networks they use. They can show you the games and other things you can do on the network. It is safer to connect online with friends you know instead of strangers.

When You Join

When you sign up for a social network, you start a **membership**. As a member, you can access the site's features. Look around. Try some of the games. Watch how the people who are using the site talk to each other. Feel free to try different social networks and see which one you like most.

Some people want to play games in a made-up world. Others want to share stories about musicians and movie stars. Social networks designed for kids try to keep users safe from strangers. One example is giantHello. On giantHello, users set up a profile page. From this page, you can upload photos, join groups based on your interests, send messages to friends, and update them on what you are doing.

It is fun to use social networks with friends. Check sites out together to find out if a social network is right for you. After you create accounts, you can meet again online.

Create a Profile

Social-networking sites ask you to create a profile. Your profile tells people about you. Do not put too many facts on your profile. Never put a picture of yourself online. Pick a picture of an object or an **icon** for your profile. It can be of something you like. It should not be a photo of you. Talk to an adult if you are not sure what kind of picture to use. Never post private information, such as your age, phone number, or address. Make sure only people you choose can see your profile.

Most sites set limits on whom you can chat with and what you can do. Some sites let you chat by either typing your own words or by picking from a list of common sayings.

Filling out a profile on a social network can be a lot of fun. Remember, never post personal information about you or your friends online.

Terms of Use

Sit down with an adult and talk about social-networking sites. Have the adult read and explain the site's rules, or terms of use. If you see anyone breaking these rules, you can block that person or report her to the site. Know where to get help in case you forget your **password** or have other problems.

Have an adult help you sign up for a social network. He can explain the rules of the site and answer any questions you have about what is and is not safe to share online.

To join most of the safest social networks, a parent or guardian has to help you create the account. You may also have to give an e-mail address where the site can send you messages to start your membership. Sites will also ask you to pick a password and **user name**. Never use your real name as your user name. Everyone on a site can see your user name.

Laws Protecting Kids

There are different types of laws that protect kids online. Some protect them from bullies and predators. Some protect privacy. In the United States, the Children's Online Privacy Protection Act (COPPA) is a law that protects the privacy of kids under the age of 13. The law states that Web sites that collect information from kids must have a parent's permission to do so. In Canada, the Personal Information Protection and Electronic Documents Act (PIPEDA) protects all citizens. It governs how private information can be gathered over the Internet. It does not have a separate rule for kids. Instead, the Canadian government tries to educate young people about online privacy.

Cyberbullying

There might come a time when you see a cyberbully while on a social network. Bullies are people who say bad things about other people and try to scare them. Cyberbullies often write messages making fun of people. Bullies may spread mean and untrue stories, too. If a bully bothers you or you see a bully picking on

Cyberbullies can hurt your feelings and make you feel alone or scared. It is important to talk to an adult if anyone does or says anything to make you uncomfortable online.

someone else, do not get into a fight. Report any cyberbullying you see to the Web site and tell an adult. Cyberbullying is against the rules on most social networks. Users who bully can be kicked off the site.

Learn how to report bullies. Being picked on or made fun of can be hurtful and scary. Do not let a cyberbully ruin your fun online.

Never Be a Cyberbully!

When you are hanging out online, you should always remember the Golden Rule. Treat other people the way you would want to be treated. Talking to someone online is the same as in person. You should always be polite. Rude or mean talk is not okay. Never be a bully. Social networks are meant to be fun places. Cyberbullying is not funny. If you have friends who pick on others, they are not being cool. They are being mean. You should report any bullying behavior to the Web site. If you see anything online that makes you feel bad, talk to an adult.

Predators Online

Online predators are people who try to trick kids into thinking they are their friends. Predators ask kids to do **inappropriate** things. Sometimes they will even pretend to be a kid.

Many kids-only social networks have security to keep bad people out. You will be less likely to run into online predators if you chat online only with people you know in real life. Never tell a stranger your age or where you live. Never agree to meet someone in person whom you have met online. Remember, you never really know whom you are talking to online. If you think that a predator is trying to reach you, tell a trusted adult right away. This adult may need to get in touch with the police.

If a predator sends you messages, remember that it was not your fault. You have done nothing wrong, even if the predator makes you feel like you are to blame.

Sign Off

You may decide that you want to leave a social network. Maybe none of your friends use it, or you have outgrown it. You will need to close your account. Some sites ask people who want their profiles erased to fill out a form. Other sites end the memberships of anyone who has not used the site for 90 days. Check your e-mail after asking to end a membership. You may need to take more steps to finish the job. If you are not sure how to leave a social network, ask an adult.

If you leave one networking site, you may want to join another. Discovering online social networks can be fun. The Internet changes every day. In July 2011, Google announced its social network Google+. Time will tell if it will become as popular as Facebook. No matter what network is popular, though, it is important that you are always safe about whom you are talking to and sharing information with.

Just because you sign up for a social network does not mean you are stuck there. If you get bored or do not like it, you can quit and join another social network.

Safety Tips

- Personal facts like your address or school do not belong in profiles. Never share this information online.

- Limit your time online to 2 hours or fewer each day.

- Have an adult use **security software** to block bad words and sites that are not meant for kids.

- Keep your passwords a secret. If someone finds out your password, change it right away.

- Ask an adult to contact a Web site right away if you see personal facts posted about you online.

- Make sure a social network is right for you before signing up.

- Always have a parent or guardian read the site's rules with you when you sign up for a social-networking site.

- Don't use a picture of yourself for your profile. Pick a picture of an object or an icon you like.

- Make a list of "Online Dos and Don'ts" to hang near your computer.

- Never post a photo online without asking an adult first.

Glossary

age requirements (AYJ rih-KWYR-ments) Rules that say how old a person must be to do something.

apps (APS) Software for a computer or mobile device that serves a single purpose, like connecting to a social network.

icon (EYE-kon) A picture that stands for something on a computer.

inappropriate (in-nuh-PROH-pree-ut) Not suitable or right.

membership (MEM-bur-ship) Being a member of something.

password (PAS-wurd) A secret combination of letters or numbers that lets someone enter something.

responsible (rih-SPONT-suh-bel) Being in control of or caring for something.

security software (sih-KYUR-ih-tee SAWFT-wer) A tool that keeps a computer or the person using it safe.

user name (YOO-zer NAYM) The name a person uses on a computer.

Index

Web Sites

Due to the changing nature of Internet links, PowerKids Press has developed an online list of Web sites related to the subject of this book. This site is updated regularly. Please use this link to access the list:

www.powerkidslinks.com/cyber/social